Tina Nahid

MOMENTS

of

Grace

Daily Reflections for the
HOMESCHOOL MOM

Dedication

This book is first dedicated to my Lord Jesus Christ who is my Rock and the source of all grace on a moment-by-moment basis.

This book is also dedicated to my beloved husband, Nami, who has been a wonderful source of encouragement on this journey.
I'm so thankful for your simple words of wisdom and support through these years.

Last but not least, I also dedicate this book to my children, Abraham, Micah and Ellie. You have been the catalyst for me seeking the Lord for His wisdom and guidance and finding His abundant grace along this journey.
While it certainly has had its trials and errors, it has also been a source of great joy that I will never regret.

2017

CONTENTS

Introduction

About the Author

Introduction

However, I consider my life worth nothing to me; my only aim is to finish the race and complete the task the Lord Jesus has given me—the task of testifying to the good news of God's grace.

Acts 20:24

First, let me say I'm a homeschool mom who lives in desperate need of grace...*every breath I take*. And the Lord has used this path of homeschooling as a tool to show me His incredible and unfathomable love and grace for me. You see, I fail. I fail daily and miserably, yet He never gives up on me.

No matter where you may be on this homeschooling journey, whether you are just starting out or have been teaching your children for 20 years, we can never know or hear too much about God's grace! Those who are veteran homeschoolers need His grace just as much as those who are in the beginning stages. We are all in need!

The truth is, none of us can do anything apart from God's amazing grace. The Hebrew definition for grace means "favor, mercy, and kindness." Without God's favor, mercy and kindness, all of our best efforts in life are doomed to ultimately fail. The "pull-yourself-up-by-your-bootstraps" mentality just isn't biblical. We need more. We must have more, in fact.

The great news is that our Father's grace is abundant and overflowing and beyond comprehension for those who trust in Jesus Christ as their Savior. As we place our hope and our trust in Him, our Father's favor, mercy and kindness is poured out to us on a moment-by-moment basis. There is no limit and no end. His grace flows over us in our worst and darkest moments, and it flows over us when we feel our very best.

In this book, my desire is to remind you, to encourage you, to instill in you that God's grace is more than enough for you. No matter what your path may look like, He is with you and for you. Your homeschooling path may look 100% different from mine. But that is perfectly fine, because His grace is more than enough for us all. We are diverse. We are unique. We are creative. And most of all we are loved. And our children are loved. And His grace is there for them exactly as it is for us.

So, let's explore deeply and drink in this abundant Living Water of grace. Let us plumb the depths of God's love through His boundless grace. And even then, we will only skim the surface at best. Yet, may we know and experience above all things that it is He who carries us daily in His arms, who loves us and our families without measure or limit. This is true when we fail and when we succeed. His grace never runs out and it never changes.

In Grace and Truth,

Tina

Worldly Wisdom vs. God's Grace

Now this is our boast: Our conscience testifies that we have conducted ourselves in the world, and especially in our relations with you, with integrity and godly sincerity. We have done so, relying not on worldly wisdom but on God's grace.

2 Corinthians 1:12

As homeschooling mothers, we have ample opportunities to rely on God's grace, instead of merely worldly wisdom. But how often do we default to the wisdom of this world instead of God's wisdom of grace? I know this mom certainly struggles with that!

When I first began my homeschooling journey, I read book after book about "how to" teach my children and "how to" be a godly parent and "how to" be a good wife, etc. I read so much that my mind felt as if it would explode! Now, don't get me wrong, I am not against reading and studying in order to attain knowledge and a better understanding. Yet, there comes a point when all the various opinions, philosophies, interpretations, and approaches can become more confusing than helpful. I realize that *when I take any one approach and try to use it as a "formula" for success, I have traded God's grace for worldly wisdom.*

Worldly wisdom espouses a formulaic approach to life. It basically says, "If you do A, B, and C, then you will get D, E, and F." Yet, is this truly what God's grace says? *Often, we as believers in Christ want a formula.* We want something that will ensure that all our efforts will pay big dividends in the long run. We want assurance that if we do certain actions, that those around us, namely our children and spouses, will be successful, happy, competent people. We want to see results, and we want to see them now!

As most of us realize, God's ways are not our ways. His ways are much, much higher and broader than ours. And the wisdom of His grace is far better and more freeing than a worldly, formula approach to homeschooling. What does walking daily in this grace look like exactly? Well, there's no formula for it, but I know it's centered on the Gospel. It is Jesus-centered. It's love-centered. It's Holy Spirit driven.

The Apostle Paul based all of His knowledge and his entire ministry on God's grace. We, as homeschooling mothers, can do likewise. Paul was raised as a scholar. He studied and studied the Torah so much that he most likely had huge portions of it memorized, if not all of it! So, I don't believe Paul would discourage us as mothers to seek wisdom through books, seminars, etc. Yet, Paul's knowledge wasn't what motivated him. It wasn't what kept him going in ministry. It was God's grace. That was powerful enough for him. And it is for us as well.

If you depend on God's grace,
there is no such thing as impossible.

—Sri Chinmoy

Walking In Our Grace Gifts

We have different gifts, according to the grace given to each of us. If your gift is prophesying, then prophesy in accordance with your faith; if it is serving, then serve; if it is teaching, then teach; if it is to encourage, then give encouragement; if it is giving, then give generously; if it is to lead, do it diligently; if it is to show mercy, do it cheerfully.

Romans 12:6-8

When I began my homeschooling journey, I read every book and article available to me in order to understand how to undertake this seemingly impossible endeavor. The concept of educating at home was so foreign to me, as I had come from a long line of public school teachers in my family. Although I found the idea of home schooling attractive, I had no clue where to begin! Thus, the books and articles began to open my understanding and helped guide me into the adventure.

Yet, too much of a good thing no longer continues to be a good thing. Slowly, I began to think that I had to copy or imitate the various authors of the books I was reading. I began to think of homeschooling in terms of a black and white formula. My thinking was, "If I organize like this, then I will be on the right track," or "if I buy this curriculum, then my children will really thrive!" I also began to think that if we did school during a fixed set of hours and a fixed schedule, then I was really going to be the Homeschool Mom Bomb!

It didn't take too long, maybe a couple of years, for me to realize that I could not sustain the homeschool journey in this capacity. And the wonderful thing that I eventually realized about God's grace is that I didn't have to! What matters is when we, as moms, use the specific gifts the Lord has given us by His grace and incorporate those into the education of our children. Am I a crafty person? Not a chance! Is it necessary for me to be? Not at all! If I have a child with a particular artistic bent, I can find outlets, classes, or activities for him/her to do on their own. The key is for us as moms to realize *our own gifting* and then use those in our homeschool for God's glory. We don't need to do it all or be it all. Our children don't need that. They need us to be who He created us to be. And that's all!

The problems come when we think we must be all the things we are not. We look at other moms and wish that we could have their gifts, instead of the ones we have. We might wish we were a musician, or a mathematician, or an artist, or whatever. Yet, that's not the way we have been gifted. It was God's decision to give us the gifts and talents we do have, and He makes no mistakes!

So, what is it you love? What is your passion? Personally, I love to read aloud to my children. I love to make different voices and animate the books. I could do this all day! But there are other areas that I am very lacking in, like math, for example. Playing a math game with my child feels like being placed in a medieval torture device! But for other moms, they excel in this area, and that is awesome!

My fellow moms, it is time for us to experience freedom in this area of our homeschooling journey. It's time for us to begin walking in the gifting we have been given, not only in other areas of our lives, but also in our home-schooling. We will see joy arise where we didn't realize it could. And we might just see our children begin to come alive in a way we never have as well.

My mother was truly my saving
grace, because she would take
me to church with her.

I would see my mother smiling in
the choir, and I wanted to know
this God that made her so happy.

If I had not had that faith
in my life, I don't know
where I would be right now.

—Tyler Perry

Under Grace

Do not offer any part of yourself to sin as an instrument of wickedness, but rather offer yourselves to God as those who have been brought from death to life; and offer every part of yourself to him as an instrument of righteousness. For sin shall no longer be your master, because you are not under the law, but under grace.

Romans 6:13, 14

Critical. Harsh. Judgmental. Demanding.

I have been all of these and more...foremost toward myself. As a new homeschooling mom years ago, I put myself under so much pressure to "perform." I just had to prove to the naysayers that I could do this, that I was capable, that I had what it took, that my children would shine, that it would all just be perfect! HA! What an illusion. I was deceived, thinking that somehow I could work hard enough and push myself and my children to "excel"; and then I would be accepted, be worthy, and that I would be justified somehow.

Can you relate to this, my friend? It has taken many years, many trials and upheavals to show me the error in that mentality. The honest truth I have found is this: **the harder I am on myself, the harder I am on others. The less grace I show myself, the less grace I show others.** Yes. It's true. If I cannot accept the scandalous and inexhaustible grace of my Father, then I cannot give that grace to my children or my husband.

Our verse in Romans tells us, today, that as believers in Christ, God's law no longer governs our lives. We are not accepted and loved based on our performance or our ability to keep laws and regulations. We are accepted and loved based on God's wonderful grace. Period. Why is this important as we homeschool our children? It's beyond easy for us to slide into a law-based mentality with our kids. We have charts, reward systems, consequences, etc. And while those are indeed helpful in order to set healthy boundaries in our lives and our children's lives, they should not be what set the course of our home life.

As we begin to ask Jesus to cause us to see ourselves through eyes of grace, we will also begin to see our children through those same eyes. Then, every encounter with them won't seem like a personal attack or offense or wrong to be righted. We will see them as the beloved of the Lord whom we are called to teach and train in humility and kindness, not force and dominance.

This walk of living in light of God's grace is a moment-by-moment choice. As we choose grace in each moment, those moments are transformed into something far more significant and beautiful than we can imagine. Jesus truly can take the messy and ugly moments and transform them into a meaningful encounter by His grace.

Grace is a power that comes in and transforms a moment into something better.

—Caroline Myss

The Grace Formula

Out of the fullness of his grace he has blessed us
all, giving us one blessing after another.
God gave the Law through Moses,
but grace and truth came through Jesus Christ.

John 1:16, 17

Whenever I start a new project or endeavor of any kind, I tend to be very idealistic about not only the final product but the process as well. My approach to homeschooling in the early years was no different. I read all the how-to books. I read the home educating philosophy books. I read the history of homeschooling, etc.—I was set! I had the idea that if I followed all these formulas or "laws" of homeschooling that it would all go smoothly, and I would certainly receive a desirable outcome of perfect children, a perfect family, and a perfect me!

How long did it take for this dream, this idealism to die a violent death? Not very long! I quickly realized that formulas do not give life. Formulas do not assure a desired outcome. And this is when it hit me that I was living a law-based lifestyle instead of a grace-focused life. Jesus did not bring us more law—He brought us grace and truth. Because of his entrance into the human race, all of humanity can now experience the unmerited and unearned favor of God. We no longer rely on rules, regulations and formulas to guide us.

This is an important truth for us as homeschool moms. Laws and formulas don't last and ultimately lead to burn out when it comes to educating our children. We can certainly have routines, schedules, guidelines and boundaries. Those are all healthy and positive and necessary. Yet, when it comes to our reliance and our source of strength and purpose, grace is at the core. Grace and truth will carry us along this journey with hope and peace. Nothing else will suffice and nothing else can take its place.

Jesus came to bring the nuance to our lives. He came and gave us His Spirit who will lead us and guide us with His still, small voice in His own particular way for our unique family. He knows what each of our children need, and only His grace can provide for those needs. The most wonderful gift we give to our children is continually pointing them to the limitless grace of their loving Creator in the midst of a hurting and chaotic world. Daily pointing them to Jesus who Himself is Grace and Truth is the greatest mission we can undertake.

Suffering, failure, loneliness,
sorrow, discouragement, and
death will be part of your
journey, but the Kingdom of God
will conquer all these horrors.
No evil can resist grace forever.

—Brennan Manning

The Humility of Grace

Likewise, you who are less experienced, submit to leaders. Further, all of you should clothe yourselves in humility toward one another, because God opposes the arrogant, but to the humble he gives grace.

1 Peter 5:5

During church service one night, I noticed my daughter on the front row sitting with her friends. She had come to church with my husband that night in his car, and I had come in a different vehicle. So, when I saw what she was wearing and how her hair looked, I immediately became angry and embarrassed. I couldn't even pay attention to the worship songs because of how she looked! I caught her eye and told her to come with me to the restroom where I proceeded to berate her about her hair and clothing. After a "good talking to" she left the bathroom with her spirit crushed. As I came back into the service and tried to sing, the Holy Spirit convicted me so strongly of my pride and the shaming of my daughter that I could barely get a word out.

Again, I caught my daughter's eye and asked her to come back beside me. I whispered in her ear that I was so sorry for my harshness and pride, and I asked her to forgive me. She began to cry silently by my side as I hugged her. Then she looked up and said, "I forgive you, and I love you too." After that, the burden in my heart lifted, and I was (tearfully) able to sing once again. This is just one of many snippets of opportunities that I have had over the many years to humble myself before my children. As parents, we can be so self-righteous toward our children at times. When they embarrass us. When they act foolish. When they make mistakes. When they sin.

Yet, true grace can only be expressed to our children when we realize just how much amazing grace we are in need of ourselves. When we step back from pride, arrogance and selfish ambitions and realize that we are not our children's judge, then freedom can truly begin for us. I think we struggle, even more, as homeschooling parents with a tendency toward this self-righteous attitude toward our children. We want them to *look the part* and to *play the part,* yet this isn't our Father's will.

May we remember to come alongside our children with humility and to extend grace to them even when they don't deserve it. Because truly, none of us deserve it. Yet we have all freely received it in Christ.

If there is one thing I have learned on this incredible journey we call life, it is this: the sign of a truly successful individual is humility.

—Naveen Jain

The Greatest Sinner

This saying is trustworthy and deserving of full acceptance: "Christ Jesus came into the world to save sinners"—and I am the worst of them.

1 Timothy 1:15

I came into the homeschooling journey with a head full of dreams, ideals, perceptions and formulas. Yes, formulas. You know, those equations that tell you that A + B = C. I read all the homeschool how-to books on the market. I watched all the YouTube videos I could find. I talked to all the veteran homeschoolers I could find. And thus my journey began with me thinking that if I just followed the formulas...all would be well, and my children would be so much more spiritual and so much better off in every way than I was—all because I chose to homeschool them!

I'm going to pause now and insert hysterical laughter at this point. LOL is all I can say! Now, if you are just starting to homeschool, please don't mistake my laughter for cynicism. Ideals are good, and dreams are great! Goals and mission statements are important. Yet I will break it to you gently, the way I wish someone would have broken it to me. Are you ready? *There is no homeschool formula for perfect children.* There. I said it.

The sooner we can dispel with this false teaching and begin to see ourselves, the parents in the home, as the greatest sinners in the home, the healthier and more peaceful our homeschool lives will be with our children. Yes, it's true! Believe me. I spent many years focusing on what I will call *Christian behavior modification* techniques for my children. And all I can say is that living that way isn't restful. It isn't resting in Christ. It is living in self-righteousness. And it doesn't produce the fruit we would hope to see in our children or ourselves.

Let us be like Paul who viewed himself as the worst of sinners in need of the most grace. In every interaction with our children, whether it is during their lessons or during dinner or whenever we interact with them, may we remember our great need of grace and therefore show that to our children through our body language, our facial expressions, our words and our actions. It will take God's grace in us to do this, but as we walk in humility with our children, the fruit will grow in which we could have never produced in our own strength.

Although my memory's fading, I remember two things very clearly: I am a great sinner and Christ is a great Savior.

—John Newton

Only Grace

But God's mercy is so abundant, and his love for us is so great, that while we were spiritually dead in our disobedience he brought us to life with Christ. It is by God's grace that you have been saved.

Ephesians 2:4, 5

Looking back to my college years and early adulthood, I can so clearly see, now, that I was spiritually dead. Though I had been brought up in church and had gone through confirmation at age 12, I had not received Christ as my Savior and did not have a living relationship with Him. Thinking back upon those days is like an out-of-body experience as I look at old photos of myself or try to remember, and all I can say is: *"Who was that person?"*

Can you relate? Maybe your experience is different than mine. And maybe our children's experiences will be different than ours was. The thing for us to know and to focus on is that God works in a variety of ways in order to bring us to salvation. My story will not be the same as yours, and our stories will most likely not look like our children's. And that's okay. We need to not only accept this reality, but celebrate it as well. How boring life would be if our Father did everything exactly the same!

The beauty of it all is that there is one common thing that saves us all...that's grace! Grace is the common saving factor that God has extended to all humankind. Whether we homeschool our children or don't, God's grace is there for us in the midst of it all. To this we cling. We don't cling to the concept of homeschooling as a means of salvation for our children. It is a choice many of us have felt led to make, and it has many benefits. But salvation isn't one of them.

So let us place our hope and trust where it should be...squarely upon the strong foundation of God's grace. And let us not be moved come what may. Let us hold on to His grace when all around us seems to be crumbling or even falling apart. His grace not only saves, but it sees us through to the very end of our earthly lives as well. It is the one constant above all.

*To be convinced in our hearts
that we have forgiveness of sins
and peace with God by grace
alone is the hardest thing.*

—Martin Luther

The Never-Ending Story of Grace

The faithful love of the Lord never ends!
His mercies never cease.
Great is his faithfulness;
His mercies begin afresh each morning.
I say to myself,
"The Lord is my inheritance;
Therefore, I will hope in him!"

Lamentations 3:22-24 NLT

This verse is among my top favorites verses in the Bible. I cannot even recount the number of times this passage has encouraged me through the years as a stay-at-home, homeschooling mother. I have often laid my head on my pillow at night thinking of all the ways I had blown it that day, yet this verse never ceased to enter my mind and assure me that tomorrow was a new day, and that God's grace was plentiful and abundant to cover every mishap.

Sometimes I question God by thinking, *"Is it really that simple, Lord? Is it really true that each morning is a new opportunity filled with fresh grace?"* I often have the notion that the Lord doesn't understand just how bad I screwed up this mothering thing today! I just can't fathom the possibility that my Father accepts me, loves me, adores me, and pours grace upon me even after I have failed so miserably.

But He continually brings me back to this truth. HE is the author of Truth. I'm not. And if HE says that His grace for me is never-ending and never ceases, then I must choose to believe it. When I choose to believe it, I am walking in faith. And that pleases Him!

So no matter what we have done during our homeschooling day, His grace is flowing toward us continually. Maybe we allowed ourselves to become embroiled in a heated debate with our teenager that led to sarcasm, shaming and yelling. Maybe we lost our patience with our elementary-aged child over their math facts. Maybe we complained about the messiness of our house to everyone within earshot. I've been there, done that, bought the t-shirt on ALL the above (many times actually). No matter what has happened, we can rest assured His grace is there. As we apologize and humble ourselves before Him and before our children, His grace floods in like a mighty river. As we set aside some time in our day just to be with Him, to seek Him, to drink in His presence He will meet us exactly where we are. He will assure our hearts of His unconditional love. And we will, in turn, be able to show forth that love to our families.

Remember it is HIS faithfulness, not ours. His faithfulness never fails. He has promised to carry us through this life by His never-ending and abundant grace. Yes, it really IS that simple. Choose to believe it, to walk in it, to revel in it today and every morning.

Our worst days are never so bad
that you are beyond
the reach of God's grace.
And your best days are never so
good that you are beyond the
need of God's grace.

—Jerry Bridges

Mission of Grace

But I reckon my own life to be worth nothing to me; I only want to complete my mission and finish the work that the Lord Jesus gave me to do, which is to declare the Good News about the grace of God.

Acts 20:24

As homeschooling parents, we are often encouraged to write a "mission statement" which consists of the reasons that we have chosen to educate our children at home. The reason for this is that it can serve as a reference point for us to help keep us on track when times get hard. And they do get hard! I have done this in the past and found it helpful.

Paul certainly gave us his mission statement in this passage of scripture. His mission was to declare the good news about God's grace to all people. When I read this, I ask myself, "Isn't this the highest mission statement any of us could have?" I believe the answer to that question is a resounding "Yes!" In our life as homeschoolers and parents, there can be no greater mission than instilling the good news of grace into our children while they are still under our roof.

Of course, we, as homeschool parents, often choose other facets of life as our mission, such as instilling good character, hard work ethic, academic ability, etc. But all of these pale in comparison to the one mission that matters the most. And that mission is sharing the good news of God's grace in word and deed, by the example of our lives each day. This is truly our highest goal as parents. If we put our hope and trust in any other area, we are most likely headed for disappointment on a grand scale!

Remember, we are to be faithful to plant the seeds of grace in our children's lives. We may not see the seeds come to fruition for many years, or we may see glimpses of fruit here and there. But we are not the Holy Spirit. He knows exactly what it will take for each of our children to experience God for themselves. Our mission is like Paul, to live out the grace-based life in front of them and leave the rest to God.

Grace, then, is grace,—
that is to say,
it is sovereign,
it is free, it is sure,
it is unconditional,
and it is everlasting.

—Alexander Whyte

Meaningful Grace

My old self has been crucified with Christ.
It is no longer I who live, but Christ lives in me.
So I live in this earthly body by trusting in the
Son of God, who loved me and gave himself
for me. I do not treat the grace of God as
meaningless. For if keeping the law could
make us right with God, then there was
no need for Christ to die.

Galatians 2:20-21

How often have you, like me, felt like the entire weight of your homeschooling journey was solely upon your shoulders? How often have you felt overwhelmed and burdened with the thought of failure or disappointment? How often have you felt the pressure for you children to perform and look good enough so you can "prove" to the outside world that homeschooling works, and that it produces perfect children?

If you can't yet relate to these struggles, you have probably just started in this adventure. Give it some time, and it most likely will happen! These thoughts will come, and when they do, I pray you remember this devotion. Run to it and read it again. Soak up this truth:

No one can homeschool well (or do anything else for that matter) without the divine grace of God working in his or her lives. If we try to do it on our own, our own way and in our own strength, we are effectively making God's grace meaningless to us. And we don't want that! Therefore, the more we lean on and depend upon His grace, the more joy and meaning and purpose there will be in our lives as homeschool moms.

Sometimes there is this pervasive attitude that if we openly confess and rely upon the sacrifice of Jesus for our behalf, and if we place our entire faith upon His grace in our lives, that somehow we are copping out or excusing ourselves from "doing our best" in life. Nothing could be farther from the truth! It's actually just the opposite. The *more* we cast our trust upon the grace of the Lord, the *more* peaceful and productive our lives will be upon this earth. The *more* we recognize and become aware of God's grace-filled presence in our day-to-day activities and routines, the *more* we enjoy our lives and our homeschool days.

May we celebrate God's gift of grace in our homeschooling journey by being unashamed of the fact that we must totally rely upon our Heavenly Father for all wisdom, guidance, help and understanding. *His grace is the single greatest asset we have when educating our children at home.* It is gloriously enough.

A state of mind that sees God in everything is evidence of growth in grace and a thankful heart.

—Charles Finney

Living Under Grace

For sin shall no longer be your master, because you are not under the law, but under grace.

Romans 6:14

Coming to a fuller knowledge of the grace of God has been a process for me on this homeschooling journey... a process that has been painfully slow at times and has involved many twists and turns along the way. It has included excursions into the land of legalism on more than one occasion.

Legalism? You may be wondering what that is. Legalism simply is when we attempt to follow God by following a set of rules. It is living based on a formula mindset. It is based on *my drive* to work hard enough, be good enough, *to somehow deserve something.*

Does this sound familiar at all? It can occur so easily that we are not even aware we have fallen into it. We are living "under the law" without understanding. Sometimes the formula tells us that if we go to a certain type of church, then we are right with God. The rule might be that if we wear certain clothing, then we will be considered more holy and righteous. Or maybe if we use a certain curriculum and say certain prayers daily or faithfully have devotions every morning, then we are doing well and then God will be pleased. Do you see the pattern? The focus of legalism is US. It's about how WE are doing and how religious WE are.

The truth is that those who call Jesus their Savior and Lord don't live under the law, but under grace. We can walk in freedom daily from the bondage of trying to be "good enough" for God. He has already made us good enough through the sacrifice of His precious Son! It's so important for us to allow this truth to take root deep down in our spirits. Walking in God's grace and love as homeschooling mothers is where we will find lasting joy. It is the way to peace for our families and us as well.

Taking the focus off of us allows us to see that our Father is so much bigger and more amazing than we had ever dared to imagine. When we say *yes* to His grace as our guiding passion, He then opens the floodgates to experiencing His Presence like never before. We begin to see fear, anxiety, and depression lifting off of our shoulders. We no longer carry the heavy weights of not feeling good enough. We can freely fix our eyes on Jesus, who is more than enough. And because *He is*, we are also.

May we open our hearts and our minds today to the ultimate gift of grace.

*I am a most noteworthy sinner,
but I have cried out to the Lord
for grace and mercy, and they
have covered me completely.
I have found the sweetest
consolation since I made it my
whole purpose to enjoy
His marvelous Presence.*

—Christopher Columbus

I Can't, But His Grace Can!

Let us then approach God's throne of grace with confidence, so that we may receive mercy and find grace to help us in our time of need.

Hebrews 4:16

How often in my homeschooling journey I have tried to "will" my way through the maze, carrying the entire load upon my shoulders in an effort to control the environment and make everything work the way I want it. How often I have been like the Little Engine that could, trudging up the long, steep hill shouting, *"I think I can! I think I can! I think I can!"* Yet, I never seemed to make it to the *"I know I can!"* part. My engine had stalled, sputtered and blown up before that point!

On the heels of this "I think I can" mentality quickly came the inevitable burnout phase. This is the phase where the daily mantra in my head went something like:

"Why bother?"
I'm not cut out for this."
"I'm a failure."
"I can't do this."

Can you relate? Chances are if you have been homeschooling for any length of time, you can. We are often taught that we can do anything we put our minds to. We are encouraged to work hard and succeed. And while there is some truth to this "American Dream" mentality, there is a far more important and foundational truth that we need to realize. The most freeing truth that we can ever experience is the truth of grace. This is the truth that tells us that God's grace is freely available to us on a daily, moment-by-moment basis. We not only come to God's salvation by His grace, but His grace is what sustains us and carries us every single day of our lives...and into eternity.

So it is with our homeschool journey as with every other area of our lives; our marriages, our parenting, our jobs, etc. It is a life of coming to God's throne and receiving His grace *continually* by His Spirit. It is recognizing that we *cannot* do it all. It is by recognizing that we *cannot* will ourselves to be all we can be. The truth is, without His bountiful grace, most days I would want to stay in bed and pull the covers over my head! The daily grind of a home educating mother's life can be challenging to say the least. I personally feel parenting and homeschooling have challenged me more than anything else in my life!

So, I want to encourage you today by telling you that God's grace is unending. It never runs out. We can run to His throne every minute of the day, and there have been many days I have done this. Truly! In fact, the more I stay in this place of total dependence upon the goodness and grace of God, the more peaceful and relaxed I am in homeschooling. Not all days do I feel like this, but more than not. And that is progress!

When we home educate our children, we will always be in need. We will need *wisdom* on how to best teach or help our children. We will need an enormous amount of *patience* and understanding. We will need a *persevering faith* to endure the doubts and frustrations. And the great news is our Savior is there to meet every need we present to Him. There is no need that He is unwilling to meet for us!

May we become well acquainted with God's throne of grace. May we learn to sit at His feet and bask in His mercy and grace for us each and every day. This is doubly true when we mess up, blow our tops, and generally want to quit (And this will happen!). It's in those times, He can draw us even closer and show us His grace in an even more powerful way than ever before. It's ALL part of the journey. The good AND the bad. Let's embrace it all.

Saving faith is an immediate relation to Christ, accepting, receiving, resting upon Him alone, for justification, sanctification, and eternal life by virtue of God's grace.

—Charles Spurgeon

Grace to Be Ourselves

But by God's grace I am what I am, and the grace that he gave me was not without effect. On the contrary, I have worked harder than any of the other apostles, although it was not really my own doing, but God's grace working with me.

1 Corinthians 15:10

In 1980, Robin Williams starred in the musical "Popeye" in which he sang a song called *"I am what I am!"* It was such a catchy song in the movie, and when I read this verse, I was reminded not only of the song but also more importantly of its deeper meaning. Popeye was expressing his individuality in a dynamic way and standing up for who he was, no matter who liked it!

In a similar way, many of us as homeschool moms must learn to accept who we are and how God wired us. We are all unique and different from each other, and this was God's plan for us. Sometimes, we can fall into the trap of wishing we had the gifts, talents and skills of another mom we know. We try to act or look like or imitate those who we admire only to find that we cannot sustain the façade for very long. And we end up burned out and feeling like a failure.

The encouragement for us from Paul today is for us to simply be who we are and to accept that. We must rely upon God's grace to fill in the gaps or weak areas of our lives and begin to not only accept ourselves as we are but to like ourselves as well. It's one thing to accept, and it's another to actually like. But we must! We cannot change ourselves. No self-help book will totally transform us into another person. That isn't our Father's will anyway! He loves us as we are and has a plan for us to fulfill with our children as well.

No matter what we may have believed to the contrary, God gave us the children we have for a reason. We are well suited, by His grace, to parent and educate these children as needed. This doesn't mean we will do it flawlessly or perfectly by any means. But His grace is sufficient to cover all our deficiencies as we trust and rely on Him daily. Let us believe this and let us sing along with Popeye, *"I am what I am and that's all that I am and I am what I am what I am!"*

Once we believe in ourselves,
we can risk curiosity, wonder,
spontaneous delight,
or any experience that
reveals the human spirit.

—E.E. Cummings

Grace, Mercy and Peace is Enough

Grace, mercy and peace from God the Father and from Jesus Christ, the Father's Son, will be with us in truth and love.

2 John 1:3

Early on in my homeschooling journey, I was very focused on the "mission" and the "purpose" of educating my children at home. I had my mind set on the hope that I was going to raise children that loved God and never strayed from the narrow path. Instead of fixing my eyes solely on Jesus, I fixed my eyes on the outcomes that I hoped for to guide me and be my motivation to keep going.

As I look back over the years, I can see that I had misplaced my hopes on to something that was fleeting, on something God never intended me to put my hope or trust in. Is it because my children have completely abandoned their faith? Not at all. But have my children turned out to be the picture-perfect role models that I had idealized in my mind? "No", to that as well.

The truth is no one could have ever lived up to the expectations I had set up in my mind of how my children *should* live and behave. My expectations were a standard that even I myself could have never attained. Not only were my expectations often unrealistic, even my realistic ones were rarely met due to the fact that my children are humans with flaws and issues of their own. They are their own individuals wholly apart and separate from me.

This is where the good news of the beauty of our verse today comes in. What is it that is promised to be with us each and every day of our lives on this earth, regardless of the circumstances?—**Grace, mercy and peace.** Three beautiful words, so simple, yet so profound. The one thing we can always count on and always cling to as we walk this homeschool walk is that our Father's grace, mercy and peace will be with us. They will be with us in truth and love. What greater promise can God give to us than this? We must let this be our guide, and we must let this be *enough*, because it truly is. And it always will be.

*Immerse yourself
in the curriculum of grace.*

—Max Lucado

Grace Upon Our Children

And the child grew and became strong;
he was filled with wisdom,
and the grace of God was on him.

Luke 2:40

Educating our children at home is a long and often arduous process. In the beginning of my homeschooling journey, I was a starry-eyed idealist who thought that by my own choice to homeschool that I could somehow *save* my children; that homeschooling them would make them more spiritually minded, wiser, and just better people in general. Now several years into it, I realize that this hope was misplaced, that this concept or teaching was false.

This is no way meant to discourage us from the pursuit of home education. On the contrary! There are many positive benefits to both our own lives and the lives of our families by following this path. My point is, though, that this path does not lead our children to salvation. It is the Lord's grace alone that does that. Just as the scriptures say that Jesus grew in wisdom, and that grace was upon him, so it is with our own children. Whether we see signs of that grace or not, it is there.

Often, we as moms can become disheartened with the outward behavior of our children, even to the point of wanting to abandon homeschooling all together. This is because we have misplaced our hope. We have placed our hope in our own attempts to control or modify our children's behavior, thereby modifying their hearts. We have the idea that if we control their environments or their friendships or what they see and hear, that somehow this will ensure that they will grow up the way we want them to. Yet, this simply isn't the truth.

The truth, my friends, is so much greater and more profound! The truth will give us a sense of peace and comfort that we could never have otherwise. This truth is the truth of God's amazing grace on each of our children's lives. What we cannot do in our own strength, and what we cannot do in our homeschooling efforts, God more than makes up for by His grace. His grace will carry our children for the long haul, beyond any influence we may have upon their lives. So, while we are faithful to carry on with our call to educate our children at home, we can leave it in our Father's loving hands to cover our children with His grace and love for the duration. He alone is able to carry them and bring them to Him.

Grace is sufficient even though we huff and puff with all our might to try and find something or someone that it cannot cover. Grace is enough.

—Brennan Manning

Grace to Laugh

We were filled with laughter,
and we sang for joy.
And the other nations said,
"What amazing things the Lord
has done for them."
Yes, the Lord has done amazing things for us!
What joy!

Psalm 126:2, 3

The routines of a stay-at-home and/or homeschool mother can become very monotonous over time. There have been times, even seasons, where it was all I could do to drag my weary bones out of bed in the morning. Not simply because I was tired, but because I didn't want to face another day of routine and the "same old, same old."

I realized a few years back that I was taking my life and myself way to seriously. When was the last time I had a good laugh? When was the last time I had rejoiced? When was the last time I just acted silly and joked around with my husband or my friends? I began to realize that I had lost my joy. I had allowed my life, my circumstances, and the routines deter me from a life of joy.

Laughter is a great medicine. I began to understand and embrace having a good time again, not always having to be the serious one who "holds it all together." Mom's night out is a great way to distress and experience a healthy dose of laughter. Gathering together to be open with our struggles and to even laugh at ourselves is emotionally good for us! If you don't have a group, start one! That's what I did, and I am so glad. Bring on the laughter!

Laughter is the closest thing to the grace of God.

—Karl Barth

Grace to Endure

Therefore, since we are surrounded by such a great cloud of witnesses, let us throw off everything that hinders and the sin that so easily entangles. And let us run with perseverance the race marked out for us, fixing our eyes on Jesus, the pioneer and perfecter of faith. For the joy set before him he endured the cross, scorning its shame, and sat down at the right hand of the throne of God. Consider him who endured such opposition from sinners, so that you will not grow weary and lose heart.

Hebrews 12:1-3

We all like to be appreciated. As moms, we often teach our children the importance of saying "thank you" in a variety of situations. As homeschooling moms, who give so much of our lives to educating and training our children, we enjoy the moments when our children express gratefulness for all we do for them.

But alas, I feel I must go ahead and break the news to you as gently as possible—our children do not always express gratefulness for educating them or for anything else for that matter! To be honest, there may be seasons where they are not only ungrateful for it, they may even resent you for doing the very thing you feel called to do.

Yes, it's true. Maybe this has never happened to you. Maybe it just hasn't happened yet. Maybe it never will. It has certainly happened to me and still happens quite frankly. But just in case it does or it has, let me encourage you with this: *Our calling is not to make our children grateful. Our calling is to fix our eyes on Jesus and do all things for His glory alone.* Is that hard? Yes, at times. Is enduring fun? Not especially. Yet, we must view homeschooling and parenting in general as more of a marathon than a sprint. It's one big, *long* adventure!

Jesus endured shame. He endured scorn. He endured hardship. Why? *For the JOY that was set before Him.* He endured because He knew He had a calling and He knew His destiny. He knew the Father's joy. *And this was enough.* So because of the perseverance of Jesus, we can rest and know that He is with us. It makes no difference if our children are not grateful to us in the short term. It may take years for them to ever express their thanks. And sadly, we need to accept that it may never happen. Yet, none of that should be our goal. None of that is our reward. *Our reward is Jesus* who is faithful to all His children all the time.

*Endurance is not just the ability
to bear a hard thing,
but to turn it into glory.*

—William Barclay

Grace That Is Greater Than All Our Sin

God's law was given so that all people could see how sinful they were. But as people sinned more and more, God's wonderful grace became more abundant. So just as sin ruled over all people and brought them to death, now God's wonderful grace rules instead, giving us right standing with God and resulting in eternal life through Jesus Christ our Lord.

Romans 5:20, 21

Oh, the plethora of behavior charts that used to cover my refrigerator when my children were young. I read so many, followed so many, tried so many until I was utterly exhausted with them! It was so frustrating because, lo and behold, my children seemed to rarely want to follow the rules! How dare they?

I used to get so fed up, so offended, so upset when my children would disobey me. It always came back to *"What am I doing wrong?"* or *"If only I was a better mom, my children wouldn't act this way,"* or *"What formula am I not following?"* What I failed to realize and truly understand was this simple truth:

My children were sinners. Profound, I know.

If we can just accept this truth about ourselves and about our children, we can avoid the harsh, over-the-top overreaction when they mess up, when they fail, when they disobey. We cannot take everything they do so personally as an affront to our identity as a mom. We can just accept that they will sin—Often!—Just as we do! We can give them consequences with a heart of love and care instead of one of condemnation and shame. We can realize that where sin happens, grace overflows even more.

This is so important for us to understand, my friends. We as moms (and especially homeschool moms who are with our children 24/7 and feel a sense of total responsibility for them) have a tendency to carry so much guilt and shame because of the bad choices our children sometimes (or often) make. We feel that we automatically must be failing if our children aren't who *we think* they should be. We assume that if we were better moms, better teachers, better examples, that our children would surely be perfect! Nothing could be further from the truth!

Each of us is born as sinners who must come to our own saving knowledge of Jesus Christ and His grace. We are all responsible before God. That includes our children. We will not be a perfect parent. We will mess up, sometimes royally. But I'm here to tell you that God's grace is greater. It is abundant. It is wider, deeper and more present than we can imagine.

Who is our children's True and Ultimate Parent? Who alone can save them, redeem them, and love them with an everlasting and unconditional love? We are here as earthly parents to nurture them, to guide them, and to help them on their spiritual journey, but it is God who showers His grace and love upon their lives and has a plan for each of them.

May we be grounded today in the truth that while our children are sinners, and while they will fail and disappoint us at times, our Father's grace abounds toward them. His love and grace knows no limits. And with this knowledge, may we be set free from the burden of guilt and shame we carry, from the perfectionism of thinking that they must look, act, and talk a certain way. May we shower them with the same grace we have been given.

My trust in God flows out of the experience of his loving me, day in and day out, whether the day is stormy or fair, whether I'm sick or in good health, whether I'm in a state of grace or disgrace. He comes to me where I live and loves me as I am.

—*Brennan Manning*

Grace Is More Than Enough

Three different times I begged the Lord to take it away. Each time he said, "My grace is all you need. My power works best in weakness." So now I am glad to boast about my weaknesses, so that the power of Christ can work through me.

2 Corinthians 12:8, 9

There seems to be a misunderstanding, or even worse, a false teaching within the homeschooling community that subtly tells us that we need to be strong, put-together, godly women who are always patient and loving with our children and always respectful to our husbands, who can do it all and never get weary or tired or burned out. This lie tells us that if anyone truly knew us and how often we failed to live up to these standards that we would be unworthy, a failure, a disgrace. This teaching also leads us to carry a load of secret shame and guilt over our shortcomings and our weaknesses.

If you are just starting your journey in the world of homeschooling, I encourage you to not fall into this type of thinking. It is unbiblical and shame-based. In fact, many churches also perpetuate these kinds of teachings, focusing so much on a "performance-based" mentality that God's grace is hardly even mentioned. The focus is on what you do, how you act, how your children act, how you dress, etc. The focus is all on the "doing" instead of simply "being."

Yet, this is directly opposite of what Paul tells us in this passage. This seems so counter to our religious sense, doesn't it? He is boasting in his weaknesses? He is boasting that he *can't* do it all and be all? Well, yes, that is exactly what he is saying. He is rejoicing in the fact that grace is so much bigger and better and far greater than anything he could do. He is rejoicing in God's promise of carrying him and using Him in spite of his weaknesses and shortcomings.

Isn't that wonderful news? Isn't that really wonderful that in spite of ourselves, the Lord can and will use us to bless our children, our families and the world around us, even when we are so far from perfect? Our Father knows our hearts. He sees the direction of our hearts, and He sees our desire to know Him, to love Him, and to follow Him. He knows our weaknesses, and He isn't shaming us for them. He is gently carrying us in the midst of them.

There is such freedom in this amazing grace! May we meditate on this wonderful truth and let it sink in deeply today. Whatever our issues may be, whatever our weaknesses, He will be sufficient. Is there an issue of a short temper? I know I have dealt with this one often. Guess what! His grace is enough! Yes, His love can cover a multitude of sins. He will pour His love over every situation when we turn to Him. Do you feel a lack of motivation?

Been there! His grace is sufficient! Seek His wisdom, and He will be more than capable!

There is nothing our Lord's grace cannot carry and redeem. NOTHING. Trust Him today in it all.

For me, every hour is grace.

—Elie Wiesel

Grace for Godliness

*For the grace of God has appeared that offers
salvation to all people. It teaches us to say "No"
to ungodliness and worldly passions, and to live
self-controlled, upright and godly lives
in this present age...*

Titus 2:11, 12

Within the church community at large, there seems to be
a pervading fear of the message of grace. The fear is
rooted in a belief that if we fully base our lives on God's
unconditional love and grace, then we will just continue
to sin without a thought! This unbiblical view of grace
could not be farther from the truth. Grace, in fact, is our
teacher. Grace is what keeps us from walking in habitual
sinful behavior and changes our habits.

Grace is truly where it all starts and ends. So, how should
this truth affect our homeschooling and our parenting in
general? Logically the more the message of God's grace
is continually lifted up and expressed toward our children, the more they will understand who God truly is
and will experience His love at a deeper level. God's
amazing grace doesn't mean that we never need to instill boundaries with our children. But it does mean that
we don't shame or manipulate them with guilt in order
to make them do what is right. We allow them to fail and

to be who they truly are, and we continually point them back to Jesus as the Source of all they need.

Often, we are afraid that if we rely solely upon God's grace that we aren't doing "our part." But within the Christian life itself, there is no "our part." Paul said that he had been crucified with Christ and that he no longer lived. It is Christ in us, doing it all! When we homeschool as believers, we can rely upon God's grace to teach our children through us. We are simply the branches connected to our Vine. He sustains all things as we abide in Him continually.

So let's throw away the misconception that grace is something to be afraid of. On the contrary, it is something to celebrate and rejoice in! There is no greater gift given to us than our salvation and the gift of the Holy Spirit to seal that grace within us for eternity. Rest in this great truth today and always.

A state of mind that sees God in everything is evidence of growth in grace and a thankful heart.

—Charles G. Finney

Grace for Every Moment

And the Word became flesh and dwelt among us, and we have seen his glory, glory as of the only Son from the Father, full of grace and truth.

John 1:14

Seldom do we talk about how lonely it can be to stay at home with your children and educate them. Sometimes it seems we are isolated from society, and we can feel like an outcast at certain times on this journey. Even with our children and family around us, we can still experience this deep sense of loneliness. And we can even begin to believe that God is far from us as well, that He really doesn't understand our struggle, and that He is unconcerned.

Nothing could be farther from the truth, my friend! John tells us that Jesus came to this earth in the flesh and lived among human beings in all the messiness of life on this planet. He knows first-hand the struggles that we experience daily while we are here. And He purposefully came to give us grace *in the midst of those struggles.* Our emotions can fluctuate from day to day making us question ourselves on every front. Yet, the truth does not change. It is absolute and fixed. *Jesus is with us in every moment of our days, even when we can't feel it.* We can be assured of this.

When we rise for another day, He is with us. When we trip over Legos in the floor, He is there. When we lose our tempers and yell at our kids, He is there. When we read to them, laugh with them, and cry together, He is there. And He is covering us with continual showers of grace through every moment. There is never a time when Jesus is distant from us if we have put our faith in Him. When we make a mistake, He doesn't withdraw. I used to think that if I blew it, that His Spirit would pull away from me. What a lie! I now know that He draws even closer in those moments to pick me up again and hold me in His arms.

So be at rest. Rest in this grace and in this truth. Jesus came to live life on this earth *with us*. And when He left this planet, He sent His Holy Spirit to be in us at all times. His presence is not only *with* us but also *inside of us*. He is not a far-off, distant and unconcerned Father. He is closer than our next breath. May you be encouraged today that in the times when it gets lonely, know that He is with you and all around you and in you at all times. *You are never alone!*

*And as grace is free, so is it sure.
Nothing can change, or alter, or
turn away sovereign grace.*

—Alexander Whyte

Foundation of Grace

For we are co-workers in God's service; you are God's field, God's building. By the grace God has given me, I laid a foundation as a wise builder, and someone else is building on it. But each one should build with care. For no one can lay any foundation other than the one already laid, which is Jesus Christ.

1 Corinthians 3:9-11

For me personally, choosing the path of homeschooling has brought both great joy and great pain. As mothers who are with our children day in and day out, we are continually building a foundation in their lives. Sometimes in this journey, we see glimpses of a strong foundation of faith being laid, and sometimes we wonder if our children are learning anything at all!

It can be quite frustrating at times, yet as Paul mentioned in his letter to the Corinthians, we are laying a foundation *by the grace God has given us.* Paul was just a man. And we are just women. We are just moms. But infused with the Spirit of grace, we can trust the Lord to faithfully lay a foundation through us for His glory and His purposes.

And just what *is* the foundation we are called to lay in the lives our children and those outside our family? It is

Jesus Christ himself! He is the foundation. As we continually lift him up in our lives and continue to point our children toward Him and His grace, we can be sure that God is laying a foundation in their hearts that will last for eternity. We may not see the fruition of their faith, possibly for many years. But we can trust God to bring about the harvest in their hearts as we faithfully build a strong foundation of faith in Christ alone.

Let us not build our lives on any other foundation but Christ Himself. Let us not build our foundation on academics or proper behaviors or legalistic rules. These are all doomed to greatly disappoint. We can be rest assured that the foundation of Jesus never will. He is faithful and true through it all.

There is a center to the Bible and its message of grace. It is found in Jesus Christ crucified and resurrected. Grace must therefore be preached in a way that is centered and focused on Jesus Christ Himself, never offering the benefits of the gospel without the Benefactor Himself.

—Sinclair B. Ferguson

Built Up in Grace

*And now I entrust you to God and the message of
his grace that is able to build you up and give
you an inheritance with all those
he has set apart for himself.*

Acts 20:32

As homeschooling mothers, we are in need of all the encouragement that we can get, aren't we? I know I am! Words of encouragement help me to press on for one more day. They are often like a refreshing drink of water when I am utterly dry and barren inside.

This verse in Acts today tells us that it is the message of grace that can build us up as we journey through this life. It's not the message of condemnation or criticism or judgment, but it's the message of grace that carries us day by day.

The message of grace lets us know that we are accepted, that we are loved, that we are enough, that we belong to Jesus.

The message of grace assures us that we have hope both now and for eternity.

The message of grace tells us that we are not alone in our homeschooling venture, but that our God is for us and will empower us all along the way.

The message of grace whispers to us that on our very worst days, we are covered by Jesus and that His mercy is new every morning. It tells us that tomorrow will be a new day.

How I never want to take the grace of God for granted! It truly provides for everything we need in this life. I believe educating my children at home has taxed my reserves and stretched me as nothing else in life has or could! And without His grace to continually build me up, I could not continue. Of this, I have no doubt.

Be encouraged today by the wonderful grace that is extended to you in Jesus Christ. Be built up in that grace, knowing that He is with you in every moment.

*And as grace is free, so is it sure.
Nothing can change, or alter,
or turn away sovereign grace.*

—Alexander Whyte

Boast-Free Grace

God saved you by his grace when you believed. And you can't take credit for this; it is a gift from God. Salvation is not a reward for the good things we have done, so none of us can boast about it.

Ephesians 2:8, 9

What a wonderful truth for us to focus on today! I don't think we can ever fully grasp the reality of this truth this side of heaven, but it's certainly worth the time to continue to explore its depths and meditate upon its beauty. Specifically in regards to our homeschooling adventure, I consider this truth to be *foundational* to all that we do on a daily basis.

Now, you may be wondering why this truth is so important to homeschooling or how this truth serves as a foundation in educating our children. Here's why. In the world of homeschooling, it's especially easy to fall into a trap of "legalism" or "formula-based thinking." I've seen it happen, and it has happened to me as well. I have not been immune to this deception.

What happens is we begin this journey with high hopes, unrealistic expectations, perfect plans and lots of formulas that seemingly promise that all will be well if we just follow the plan, the rules, then everything will go smoothly. We also begin to perform these "works" by our own strength and sheer will power. "I will make this work!" is our mantra. If our children are turning out particularly successful according to the world's standards (or even the church's standards) then we give ourselves a pat on the back for a job well done. Likewise, if our children are failing, faltering and making bad decisions, then we heap that guilt upon ourselves as well and resolve to figure this thing out and "do better."

It seems we often start out in our Christian journey understanding that it is ALL God's grace that saves and carries us. But somewhere along the way, we pick up the "works mentality" and begin to believe that it's up to us to carry it all out, that it's all based on what we do or don't do that ultimately matters. If we do well, we believe we have somehow "earned" our salvation in a way, which makes us very critical and judgmental of others who do things differently than us.

The good news is none of us can boast. Being in Christ means you live in a "boast-free zone." When we do well, it's all grace. When we fail, it's all grace. Because it's all about Jesus and what He's done, not what we have done for ourselves. So be encouraged today in the wonderful truth that you are saved, you are loved, and you will be carried until the end of your journey on this earth *entirely* by God's holy grace. Be free in that today and enjoy the gift.

*The burden of life is
from ourselves,
its lightness from the
grace of Christ
and the love of God.*

—William Bernard Ullanthorne

ABOUT THE AUTHOR

Tina Nahid has been a busy stay-at-home, homeschooling mom and wife and has 3 children. She is very active within her local homeschool support group and desires to encourage other moms on their journey. She has a M.A. in English and has had devotions published in a variety of publications over the years. Tina enjoys reading, writing, date nights with her hubby, traveling, mom's night out, exercising, mission trips and field trips with her kids.